T0195898

THE UNIVERSITY OF INSECTS

Johnson F. Odesola

authorHOUSE®

AuthorHouse™
1663 Liberty Drive
Bloomington, IN 47403
www.authorhouse.com
Phone: 1 (800) 839-8640

© *2020 Johnson F. Odesola. All rights reserved.*

No part of this book may be reproduced, stored in a retrieval system, or transmitted by any means without the written permission of the author.

Published by AuthorHouse 12/23/2019

ISBN: 978-1-7283-4131-6 (sc)
ISBN: 978-1-7283-4132-3 (e)

Print information available on the last page.

Any people depicted in stock imagery provided by Getty Images are models, and such images are being used for illustrative purposes only. Certain stock imagery © Getty Images.

This book is printed on acid-free paper.

Because of the dynamic nature of the Internet, any web addresses or links contained in this book may have changed since publication and may no longer be valid. The views expressed in this work are solely those of the author and do not necessarily reflect the views of the publisher, and the publisher hereby disclaims any responsibility for them.

KJV
Scripture taken from The Holy Bible, King James Version. Public Domain

NIV
Scripture quotations marked NIV are taken from the Holy Bible, New International Version®. NIV®. Copyright © 1973, 1978, 1984 by International Bible Society. Used by permission of Zondervan. All rights reserved. [Biblica]

GENERAL OVERVIEW OF THE FACULTIES

There be four things which are little upon the earth, but they are exceeding wise: The ants are a people not strong, yet they prepare their meat in the summer; The conies are but a feeble folk, yet make they their houses in the rocks; The locusts have no king, yet go they forth all of them by bands; The spider taketh hold with her hands, and is in kings' palaces'- Proverbs 30: 24 – 28 KJV

From the quoted Bible reference, the faculties in the University of Insects include:

1. ANTS
2. CONIES
3. LOCUSTS
4. SPIDER

These four beings are very small but they are wise. We must learn from what they portray. The **ANT** prepares **for** the future not **in** the future. This is the wisdom from the Ants. You cannot succeed by manufacturing your weapon in the battle. One of the major reasons why people fail in their relationship is that they enter into the relationship without adequate preparation – Inadequate preparation is responsible for failure even after marriage is contracted. A lot of people prepare for the wedding without preparing for the marriage. Wedding is for one day, marriage is for life, so one important lesson from the Ant is preparation.

The second insect is the **CONY**. Conies teach us where to build. Where you build on matters. They build on the rock and the foundation of any house is very important. Psalm 11:3 KJV- If the foundation be destroyed, what can the righteous do?

The foundation of the building is the most important part of the building even though it is not the most beautiful part of the building. The foundation needs not to be beautiful to be durable. The foundation needs not be beautiful to be valuable but it has to be strong. So the first lesson is Preparation, the 2nd lesson is having a "Solid Foundation".

The Third is the **LOCUST**. What do they do? They move together in bands. This means they network, strategize and collaborate. They have the essence of team spirit. The word of God says, "They that work with the wise shall be wise." – Prov. 13:20 KJV. Be not deceived evil communication corrupts good manners.

From Locusts we see the importance of discovery; the discovery of your band or your people or your group or your team or your network and making sure that you associate right.

A wise man once said where you will be in 5years will be determined by the books you read and the friends that you keep – The books you read: INFORMATION, The friends you keep: ASSOCIATION. So, your **INFORMATION** and your **ASSOCIATION** determines your **DESTINATION.**

In order for you to be successful you have to be careful of the information and association you expose yourself to. Look into your life, all the negative decisions you have made and negative choices you have made was directly or indirectly connected to the association that you were involved in at that time; so your association matters a lot.

The fourth Creature is the **SPIDER.** This is a particularly small insect but it finds its way into palaces. Spiders do not to buy web in the market but everything that the Spider needs to spread a web is in the spider. The wisdom from the Spider is to let you know that there is something in you that can take you to the palace if you can just discover what you carry. If you can discover what have, if you can discover what is inside of you and focus on developing and deploying the deposit of God in you, there is no palace that cannot accept you.

Having seen these four things as a background, you now need to understand there are different kinds of people, virgins, singles or married just like there are different kinds of insects and animals.

There are singles that are wise and singles that foolish. There are married people that are wise and there are married people that are fools. The story of the Ten Virgins tells us more, Matthew 25:1-11 KJV. The issue of purity was settled, they were all righteous. So the story line was not on righteousness because they were all righteous, but the story was on Wisdom. Even though they were virgins – five were foolish, five were wise. So, you can be Holy and foolish, you can be righteous and foolish. You can be pure and foolish. This is what the Bible is talking about. Applying this to relationships, many people in the church are naive when it comes to relationships.

A lot of Christians have been messed up when it comes to relationships because they think all they need to have is spiritual power, spiritual understandings. There is a place for that but you need to understand that if you are holy and foolish, you will not be able to enter into where God wants you to enter into. Wisdom is very important.

'Get wisdom, get understanding: forget it not; neither decline from the words of my mouth. Forsake her not, and she shall preserve thee: love her, and she shall keep thee. Wisdom is the principal thing; therefore get wisdom: and with all thy getting get understanding'- Proverbs 4:5-7 KJV

There are single and married people that are wise and by wisdom have excelled. There are single and married people that have not been able to attract the type of value they desire simply because they are foolish. They do not have what they need to have. When you look at different types of things in life, you will observe that there are ratings that are given to different sectors of the world or different aspects of life in order to be able to depict their value. For example, when you see a General in the Army, you would want to know whether he is a one, two, three, four or five Star general. This will reveal their story and journey.

Stars are value rating in life and in various sectors. There are Airlines that have five Stars rating and the ones that have lesser ratings. Hotels also have Star ratings. There are five Stars, three Stars or two Stars hotels. In Dubai there is a seven Stars hotel.

There are hotels where you cannot have bad dreams. In football, Manchester United, Man City, Chelsea, for example, are the top rated football teams. Several people want to associate with these teams. But in that same premiership, we have the Blackburn Rovers and Wolgan Atlantic. Not many people identify with them or wear their symbols. Even in the Spanish La Liga, there are top rated teams like Real Madrid and Barcelona but there are also low rated teams people don't reckon with.

When we talk about Star, whether it is in Football, Music or Fashion, you have people that are rated high because of the value they carry. Those that are 5 Star Christians, 5 Star Singles, and in 5 Star marriages are valuable Christians, Valuable singles, and Valuable marriages. These are people who have come to the point where all Stars that are supposed to be in place are there – Five Stars that make you valuable and make you a valuable single or make your marriage valuable.

CHAPTER TWO

RELEVANT AND COMPULSORY COURSES

SPIRITUAL COURSE

'If the foundations be destroyed, what can the righteous do?'- Ps 11:3KJV

Your spiritual relationship with God is very important when you are married. There is a spiritual relationship you need to have with God and His word. You need to understand the word of God.

- You need to understand the power of prayer
- You need to understand the power of the word
- You need to understand the power of praise and worship
- You need to understand the power of loyalty and commitment

- You need to understand the power of order and authority
- You need to understand the power obedience

When you have a spiritual problem, you need a spiritual solution. Money will fail in this regard. Nothing can take care of spiritual matters except God. That is why you need to imbibe the spiritual aspect of these lessons.

When a lady faces constant jilting and disappointment in her relationships, there is a spiritual undertone. It is not normal for a suitor to back out of a relationship shortly before wedding. There is the story of a lady that was disappointed right on the wedding day. She was in her wedding gown waiting in church! The brother did not show up. The ceremony was cancelled eventually. This is a terrible spiritual attack. You need spiritual stamina to stop the devil from embarrassing and harassing you.

Another lady suffered a serious setback in her relationship. After the invitation was out, she got a scratch in her private part. The pain degenerated until she got married eventually. As a result of this, the newlyweds could not consummate their marriage sexually. On the third day, the husband told her in plain terms, '*you deceived me*'.

Listen to me, there are devils in the church. Deceit is a commonplace attitude. Everyone in church is an actor, the real you is at home. It takes spiritual stamina to discern sincerity from deceit. You need to be spiritually grounded in Christ. You need to have sharp spiritual eyes. Apostle Paul exercised spiritual discernment to know that the damsel that cried after the ministerial crew saying '*These men are the servants of the most high God, which show unto us the way of salvation*' is a demonic agent.

EMOTIONAL COURSE

You need to be emotionally mature. There are people who are spiritually strong but they are emotionally daft. I call them spiritual giants but emotional dwarfs. Such people do not have emotional control. They are always suspicious, sniffing around as if every other person is not spiritual. In a relationship, such a person will be seen searching his fiancée's hand bag to discover something. He would call her several times in a day to find out where and with who she is.

This spiritual giant but emotional dwarf has become a monitoring spirit by this attitude. He is jobless sort of because if he is actually busy, he will not have the time to sniff around or place a call through several times a day to monitor her. This is pure manipulation. May you grow up to become mature emotionally.

'When I was a child, I spake as a child, I understood as a child, I thought as a child: but when I became a man, I put away childish things'- 1 Cor. 13:11 KJV.

Your level of speaking, action and taking responsibility is very important prior marriage. Some men are on the lookout for a woman that will *'respect me, listen to me, and be there for me'*. The woman too is looking for a man that will *'take care of me, supply my need, lavish money on me'*. Whereas, the real issue of marriage is to fulfill the plan and purpose of God, people trivialize it. Let us be emotionally stable and mature. Only then can we handle weighty matters.

MENTAL COURSE

Christianity is not stupidity. It is not by education but by revelation. In developing your mental capacity, you need education.

Some people have a pathetic mental attitude. They know all the names of footballers, their positions in the field and their clubs. They know all match fixtures, dates, wins and loses. Their real problem begins when they are required to translate their mental capacity to pass examination.

As a Christian, you must not be stupid. Develop your mental capacity. Read books. Use the library. Take short and specialized courses. Attend seminars. Go for excursions. Be exposed. Learn modern and conventional way of doing things. Don't be naïve. If you remain in mediocrity, you will never excel in life and ministry. How can you have cooperate job without cooperate certificate. If you jump up, you will certainly come down but if you grow up you will stay up – Grow up my friend.

SOCIAL COURSE

You can be a Christian and be socially relevant. Christianity is not an enrollment for stupidity or mediocrity. Some ladies look like their grandmother: saggy, flabby and shapeless. They are like amoeba. Others look like masquerades due to excess make up. They have no sense of modesty. You need to be moderate according to the prescription of the Bible. Let your adornment be the hidden man of the heart, in that which is not corruptible, even the ornament of a meek and quiet spirit, which is in the sight of God of great price.

Be decent in your dressing. There is sense in decency. How you dress is the way you will be addressed. Stop dressing like a whore! Get those miniskirts out of your wardrobe. Close up your cleavages. Dump your see through outfits that reveals your panties. You are not for sale! Are you? Be socially relevant but don't neglect decency. Those hot dresses will land you in the hot place. Don't dress to admire randy men who will court, use and dump you like a piece of rubbish.

Some brothers are like a rainbow that has seven colours - Green trouser, yellow Shirt, purple jacket, blue socks, white tie, brown shoes, black belt. Are you from this planet or mars? Be cooperate in your outlook. Have a decent colour combination. Use the mirror before you walk out of the house.

Hello brothers and sisters, can you cook? Young man, learn how to prepare food. Young damsel, learn to cook so that you will not be giving your husband burnt offerings and salted sacrifice. Be trendy in the kitchen. Learn continental dishes and recipes. Learn to use the fork and knife properly. Don't be a misfit when you get to intercontinental dinner. Some people get confused in the public when food is served. They look mysterious as if they are saddled with the responsibility to fly a plane like a pilot. What you don't learn now will disgrace you when you get to public places. Learn and keep learning.

Are you computer literate? You need to be updated in this regard. The malady of today is that many youth cannot write but are proficient only in abbreviation. Don't be abbreviated. Write in the conventional way. Train yourself to write legibly. Some people's hand writing is like Greek or Hebrew. It is like the scribbles of a fowls legs on a wet soil. Improve your hand writing ability.

Do you have driver's license? Do you have travel passport? Travel and be exposed. Some people are born in a place, for example, Lagos where they grow, to school, get a job, marry, live and die. Not so my brethren. Travel to places and be versatile in knowledge. You can choose to be a local or global champion. Even if you have money and you are not exposed, you will still be local. Be global, don't be local.

PHYSICAL COURSE

There are several people working around who are not fit. Physical exercise profit little. Please take care of yourself do exercise, eat well. Do you know that some people have mouth and body odour. Some people avoid you because of odour, some their undies are dirty and their hair stinks.

Some ladies and gentlemen smell like he-goats. Use cologne. As a boy, do a clean shave. Don't be unkempt. Look good and mature. Visit the dentist and scrub out those green and brown colours from beneath your teeth. Wear singlet to contain your sweat and change it every day. Wash your clothes well. Dry and iron them properly. Don't leave the house in rumpled dresses. Wear good shoes.

Shave your armpits and keep them clean. Don't pick your nose in the public. There is a way a woman sits or walks. Observe these ethics. There is a way a woman enters a car, keep to this style. Move well, carry yourself very well. Your body carriage is as important as your spiritual carriage. They both have their place in your overall fulfillment in life. Tattoo is not what you should be involved with as a believer. Follow the steps of our Master, Jesus Christ. Even the cooperate world frowns at tattoo!

FINANCIAL COURSE

You have to be financially strong. Financial literacy will be very beneficial to you. You must know that money is a very good slave but a bad master. You need to know that money is not a thing you look for but a thing you work for or make to work for you. Some people at 25, 30, 35 years are still under the care of their parents. They are still under the care of their elder ones. You need to understand the intrigues of money. Money is generated for services rendered. Stand up and do something!

'And he shall be like a tree planted by the rivers of water, that bringeth forth his fruit in his season; his leaf also shall not wither; and whatsoever he doeth shall prosper'- Psalms 1:3 KJV

God is committed to bless you but you must be engaged in doing something. He blesses nothing but the thing you do. What are you doing? Are you sit at home idle or move from place to place like the devil without any definite agenda? Find something to do and do it well. An idle hand is the devil's workshop. Start up and grow up!

Some ladies harp on the fact that there is NO ROMANCE WITHOUT FINANCE. This may be true but as a lady, you need to be financially independent too! Free yourself from the bondage of the man's pocket or wallet. Many ladies want an already made man; a man that has a car, good job, house and plenty money. You too can be rich!

Don't be an acquisition. The quality of the life that the man finds in you will determine your worth to him. Don't be a dependant; also bring something to the table. Do what you can do now. Do you have a bank account? Do you have a job? Do you have a plan? Do you have a business? Make sure that you are doing something that generates money. Responsibilities have a way of increasing. Be prepared to be more responsible and responsive.

Know this: Money answereth all things

Know this: Money is defence

Know this: Money is power

Know this: money the wheel of the gospel

Know this: the gospel flies on two wings: anointing and money

Know this: God takes pleasure in the prosperity of the saints

Know this: Money has no gender bias or discrimination.

Know this: You deserve to have plenty money too!

MORAL COURSE

There are three legitimate passions in the life of any man.

- Passion for Food
- Passion for Power
- Passion for Sex

It has been said that hunger is the strongest human emotion. If you are feeling hungry, you will do everything legitimately possible to find food. It will not matter to you whether the job is a menial job. You will do it just to survive. One thing you will not do as a genuine believer is to steal or prostitute your body.

Again passion for power is generic. We all want to exercise power and authority. We want to be in control. We like to give orders and be obeyed. But we do not join a terrorist group in order to have and exercise power. We rather work to acquire power legitimately. It is either we go to school, get good job, rise to the top of the power ladder or get plenty money. You will exercise power when you have money.

Sex is a strong emotion second only hunger. Just as you are able to manage passion for food and power, you can manage the sex passion. Sex organ is not your organ but your mind. Sex begins in the mind. Bring a 90-year old naked woman and you will not have an erection.

In your mind, you will be put off immediately. It is your mind that controls the sex emotion.

Now, take this moral course: manage your sexuality well. Close the door of sex in your mind if you are single. Open the door only to your spouse if you are married. Think the right thoughts. Clean up your collections by removing all pornographic materials. Listen to only godly music and messages. Control your television channels and internet surfing. Choose morally upright friends. You will conquer the power of sex until you can legitimately exercise it within the ambits of marriage.

CHAPTER THREE

THE FACULTY OF ANTS

ANTS, although tiny creatures and most times seen as pests, are one of the most hardworking, diligent and focused creatures on earth. The life of the ant is a lesson on how to consistently succeed. Ants know that time is precious, so they value and make good use of every moment of their time. Time is the foremost resource you can exchange for value. It is life's most priced asset, do not waste it.

Principle 1

Ants are daily driven by vision and purpose only. Ants compared to other insects always set their goals. Purpose is what shapes everything that an ant does. They never work alone. Ants never wait for a leader to command and wait for a leader to tell them what to do. Like soldiers, ants knows that things they have to do.

The roles they have to perform and the roles. This kind of insect has their own way of communication and what makes them excel among others is because they never forget to follow and complete their own responsibility. They finish work before anything else.

If you have read the story about the ant and the grasshopper, you can tell that we are a lot like the green insect. There are numerous things that hinder us from focusing on one matter and completing. One reason why some do not reach their goal. If only we focus on taking on step at a time, focusing on what should be done at the moment, we shall be able to balance and get to the finish line.

Principle 2

Ants work as a team. You should have noticed ants falling in line as they collect goods. They mostly never work alone. They work in a group, in a team.

In order for you to achieve anything meaningful and experience consistent success in life in all your chosen fields, it is true that we shall choose the people we are working with, spending our time with. We should learn how to choose the right people who surrounds us, choose the right friends who would lead you to the right path and get the right support you deserve to achieve your dream. You need the right people, the right support system, and the right friends. You have to be in the right relationships!

Principle 3

Ants know when to work hard and when to rest from work.
For sure, all creature would want to rest when they already need to
rest. They know when to go out and collect their goods and they
know when it is not the right time.

Just like ants, we shall set our goals and make sure we have a
game plan to make it to the finish line.

Principle 4

Ants are small but they think big! Ants could be very small but
when they work, they work together as one. When you see an ant
looking at a piece of bread, you will realize that even if the bread
is too heavy, too big, surely they can make sure that they can their
pieces home and save it for drought.

No matter how small you think you are. No matter how small
the things you can do, it will matter, and it is still a success. You still
made it! We only have to think big! We only have to work hard and
give our best!

Principle 5

Ants prepare ahead. Compared to humans, ants do not
procrastinate. They will never settle a season without preparing.
When the sun is up, they surely will hustle and make sure they have
save themselves food when the rainy seasons come.

We should then stop procrastination!

Principle 6

Ants carry only workloads that they can handle. They may seem small to the eyes but they are the strongest insect and can carry more than their own weight.

It's amazing how other people can carry so much weight and still keep their chins up. Some people may have not realized how much they can take, but for sure when we do we would be able to accomplish every goal we have set. With strength and belief in ourselves, we can do anything.

Principle 7

As ants work together, they make sure that they look after each other. Observe group of ants surrounding one dead ant, they would even carry the body of their brother. Usually, when one of the ants are bothered, their line would break up to notify everyone that danger is coming.

Like humans, we need companions – we need family and friends. No man is an island. And surely, support system would be a great help. It is never a weakness to accept others' offer to help, thus, this will make you better, and this will make you stronger.

Ants and Humans are great comparison. Human could be such procrastinators, human can be lazy. But of course, it only needs realization for us to make ourselves better and it shall happen to everyone. It will happen to everyone.

[Please visit https://www.pressreader.com/nigeria/the-guardian-ni geria/20171026/282127816727018

For more information.]

CHAPTER FOUR

THE FACULTY OF CONEYS

The Coney in Hebrew is called shaphan. The Coney is "the hider". It is an animal which inhabits the mountain gorges and the rocky districts of Arabia Petraea and the Holy Land. "The conies are but a feeble folk, yet make they their houses in the rocks" (Pro. 30:26; Psa. 104:18 KJV). They are gregarious (fond of company; sociable; living in flocks or colonies), and "exceeding wise" (Pro. 30:24 KJV), and are described as chewing the cud (Lev. 11:5; Deut. 14:7 KJV).

A Coney is a rabbit, especially the common domesticated European rabbit.

Hyrax Small Mediterranean mammal: a small gregarious plant-eating mammal that resembles a rabbit with short ears and has toenails resembling hooves. Hyraxes live around the Mediterranean Sea and in southwestern Asia.

'The high mountains belong to the wild goats; the crags are a refuge for the coneys'- Ps 104:18, NIV

'The coney, though it chews the cud, does not have a split hoof; it is unclean for you'- Lev 11:5, NIV

'However, of those that chew the cud or that have a split hoof completely divided you may not eat the camel, the rabbit or the coney. Although they chew the cud, they do not have a split hoof; they are ceremonially unclean for you'- Deut. 14:7 NIV

It is so amazing to know that a Coney would want to live a tough life when it has a choice to be somewhere safer – to a flat land. They live in small spaces, in areas some animals would not want to live either to keep themselves safe. Can you imagine such small creatures defending themselves against very large predators? They could die anytime! This is of the reasons why they choose to live faraway and more uncomfortable than others, as much as they want to get easy food and life in a flat land, they also are wise enough to think about saving their lives by hiding/living on the crags.

Lessons from the Coneys for man are as follows:

1. *You can be small or big but it wouldn't matter. The size of your belief in God will do.*

   - Where you are from and the culture you live does not matter
   - Your skin, your tradition, the language you speak does not matter

- You past does not matter.
- The wise thought of the Coneys is to keep themselves safe in a place where predators will not think of preying on them
- Your ideas, your experiences, your thoughts matter more than the kind of family you are from
- Holding on to the Belief on God matter

'If you can'?" said Jesus. "Everything is possible for him who believes'- Mark 9:23, NIV

'I can do everything through him who gives me strength'- Phil 4:13, NIV

2. ***You will succeed!***

- The Coneys plan is to keep themselves safe from the predators. They think it is better than falling from the steep mountains because they do not fear heights.
- Always believe on yourself. You can make it!
- God will never leave you. He will always be beside you in your journey.
- You are destined to be successful. All left, is for you to believe that success in you will happen.

'And teaching them to obey everything I have commanded you. And surely I am with you always, to the very end of the age'- Matt 28:20, NIV

'You will be blessed in the city and blessed in the country'- Deut. 28:3, NIV

'The LORD will send a blessing on your barns and on everything you put your hand to. The LORD your God will bless you in the land he is giving you'- Deut. 28:8, NIV

3. *You can survive if you know you are able to provide*

- Nothing is impossible for a person who knows he can make it possible
- Your actions define life's reactions
- Your mind create life decisions, and your decisions motivate your perception for reactions.
- Goals are achieved when we believe we can with determination and passion.

'If you can'?" said Jesus. "Everything is possible for him who believes'- Mark 9:23, NIV

'See, I am doing a new thing! Now it springs up; do you not perceive it? I am making a way in the desert and streams in the wasteland'- Isa 43:19, NIV

4. *No hindrance can pin you down.*

Like the Coneys, they have understood their weakness. And so, they have made it a part of their strengths. Same with us, we have to confront our fears, our weaknesses, understand them as we make them the bricks in the castle we are making.

- You are son of God. A problem solver. Mountain mover.
- God will never give you a problem you can never resolve.
- A problem can neve

'See, I will make you into a threshing sledge, new and sharp, with many teeth. You will thresh the mountains and crush them, and reduce the hills to chaff. 16 You will winnow them, the wind will pick them up, and a gale will blow them away. But you will rejoice in the LORD and glory in the Holy One of Israel'- Isa 41:15-16: 15, NIV

'For everyone born of God overcomes the world. This is the victory that has overcome the world, even our faith. 5 Who is it that overcomes the world? Only he who believes that Jesus is the Son of God'- 1 John 5:4-5: 4, NIV

5. *Identify, Accept, Understand, Overcome Challenges*

The insects understood their difference and their weakness and never complained. They knew it was something that was destined to happen, instead, they have overcome their weakness and lived safely.

- You are not perfect. Do not pin yourself down. You are a son of God.
- Your size does not matter. What will matter will be the size of your dreams and the things you do to achieve them.
- If the Coneys have overcome theirs. We can too! It is surely not going to be as easy but it will worth it!

'For everyone born of God overcomes the world. This is the victory that has overcome the world, even our faith. 5 Who is it that overcomes the world? Only he who believes that Jesus is the Son of God'- 1 John 5:4-5; 4, NIV

6. ***Keep the positivity even on the most negative times life brings you***

- A positive man always rules the day!
- A mind filled with love, faith, and passion. Is a mind of a successful person!
- Always be positive! Expect that even if life throws you difficulties, you can still make it!
- Never submit to hardship! A successful person will never give up! Keep the faith.
- Positivity are for determined minds.
- Keep faith in yourself! Surely, a feast is ready for your success

'I can do everything through him who gives me strength'- Phil 4:13, NIV

7. ***I'm Possible. Not Impossible.***

- Your feet does not fit another shoe size. Everyone goes through different issues but everyone can make it.
- Let positivity run through your veins!

`If you can'?" said Jesus. "Everything is possible for him who believes'- Mark 9:23, NIV

[Please visit http://www.jfoutreach.org/archives/archives/lessons fromthefourlittlecreatures.pdf

To know more]

CHAPTER FIVE

THE FACULTY OF LOCUSTS

Could locusts possibly have any wisdom for us? The migratory locusts in Proverbs are the ones that get mean. They are genetically programmed to change when they are under great stress, like during a great rain after drought. During all that period of drought before the stress, locusts live solitary lives. It is the solitary phase or stage of the locust.

The swarming strains live in very inhospitable terrains like the deserts of the Middle East. About 100 years ago, scientists measured a swarm of locusts across the Red Sea, 2000 square miles of locusts. Forty to fifty square miles of solid locusts. Scientists call it the gregarious phase. The Bible calls it a plague. When they swarm, they are in their gregarious phase, and they remind us of their wisdom: "they have no king but they can stay together in bands." It's the lesson of teamwork.

God made the desert locust a special creature with a changing personality. It teaches you a valuable lesson about success and happiness in life. Ordinarily very reclusive and solitary, this animal minds its own business, ventures about only at night, and meets other locusts only for brief mating encounters. However, when the situation calls for it, they change dramatically in color and even more drastically in social behavior, becoming very friendly and group oriented, creating huge swarms for their mutual benefit.

The desert locust usually lives a very lonely, quiet, individual, and solitary life. They are extremely shy except for their brief mating encounters. They fly at night and avoid each other, very content at being alone. Rather sluggish by nature, they are quite harmless. But when put in a crowded situation with other locusts, due to ideal ecological circumstances or the search for food, they drastically change to become very social creatures.

Scientifically, a locust with its individualistic and reclusive temperament is called solitarious. When it undergoes its great personality change and becomes a very eager social creature, it is scientifically said to be gregarious! We use the word ourselves to describe someone who is very friendly, social, interactive, and enjoying group activities!

Loners are losers, God has created a woman beside of a man because he knows human potential grows higher when we are together. We shall work in team to achieve our goals. Accept help from others and return the assistance they provide.

Regardless of how you feel about others, you cannot do nearly as much or as well by yourself, as you can with the assistance of others. And you will be a whole lot happier in the exchange, for there is great pleasure in the group dynamics of saints, especially when assisted by the power of the Holy Spirit (Ps 133:1-3 KJV). Let God and the locusts be true!

How about you, do you have a locust's wisdom?

[Please visit <u>https://www.theologyofwork.org/the-high-calling/blog/lesson-locusts</u> for more information]

CHAPTER SIX

FACULTY OF SPIDER

Spiders may not be your taste (has anyone ever even tasted one?). They may not appeal to you, but they can certainly teach you a few life lessons

- Ants are in the field; but spiders in houses
- They creep into houses and make themselves at home – even though not welcomed
- They even get into King's palaces! They spin a web out of their own bowels!

Like them or not, tiny or giant, spiders are incredibly powerful and awe-inspiring. If you ever get a chance, watch how a spider spins its web.

Nature at its most awe inspiring. That's what spiders do. They build webs. They are master engineers and they create engineering miracles.

What do humans do? They dream. But only a few of them go on to make their dreams come true. Will you make your dreams come true? What will it take for you to be the engineer of your life? Here are some life lessons spiders can teach you about achieving your dreams:-

1. ***Get up! Start Hustling!***

A spider never chooses a good location, rather, when they see an opportunity, they will start weaving. They know they could not waste time as they're prey (goal) are close to them.

So get up, and start fixing yourself to start life!

2. ***Believe you can do anything and believe on what you can do.***

A spider's web is obviously fragile. Spiders know that. They know the limitations on what they can do but does not change the fact that they can do as many as they can when the first try they do falter.

3. ***Dream Big, Work Big***

It is impressive how big a web can be from a small insect like a spider. For sure, that big web started from a big dream, a big passion and a big hard work!

4. *Keep going in life*

The web is clearly a lesson in perseverance, the web can be easily destroyed but a Spider knows they can still create a new one when one does not work.

5. *Hard work pays off*

I am not sure how long it takes for a spider to complete their web. Spiders should have taken their time just to complete their work. Their efforts should have been all exerted, you see how small they are and how large their goals are. They know that even if one gets destroyed, they can still make another one! What a perseverance!

6. *Alone time is helpful*

We all know spiders build themselves alone. It something that we can do to. We are lucky though, in nature we have people behind us to support us.

7. *Give your best in every performance*

Make things extra! We are all unique in our own ways, own talents, own skills. All we have to do is nurture the nature in us.

8. *Do not be affected by the norm*

Never seek approval from anyone except God. Our job as humans are to help each other. It is God's job to judge us.

9. *Work Hard Everyday*

There is no day when we stop working. We strive hard everyday. We work hard everyday. Like spiders, there are no days that they stop weaving, it is their way of living.

As per us, we strive everyday, we work hard for ourselves and our family. So many reasons for us to keep working and for sure, the juice is worth the squeeze.

10. *Try and Try Until you Achieve it*

You will never know if you can make it unless you try again after failing.

In the same way, you too can start again – learn from your experience, remember the lessons learnt and next time, do it even much better.

11. *Life is Difficult but Worth living*

Life is never easy but that does not mean that we will stop living life. It only means that every difficulty makes us a better person. Every difficulty makes us stronger to face bigger challenges and of course bigger success.

12. *Interrelated*

We have to learn to be mindful of what we are doing. We should know what our actions can lead us to because even the smallest action can lead to big results and consequences.

13. *Leave a Legacy*

Like a spider weaving, they leave extraordinary art in the extraordinary effort they give in completing their task.

Why not be extraordinary?

14. *Get to the Finish Line!*

Remember to always take your time, weave one web at a time. Give all your best out. Prove yourself to only yourself. Let a spider be an inspiration that there is nothing that could hinder us from getting to the finish line and getting that gold!

[Visit https://www.arvinddevalia.com/blog/2010/10/05/10-lessons-from-a-spider-about-achieving-your-dreams/ to know more]

What is Kaizen Principle?

1. If past ideas have not worked, throw them away and create a better one to help you reach success.
2. Follow the Golden Rule – we shall not oppress other if we do not want to be oppressed
3. Never say never! Always keep the positivity!
4. Small success is still A SUCCESS!
5. Accept when you are wrong and correct them immediately
6. Always think of the idea before thinking about the money. Mind over Money.
7. Never stop until you know the reason why'

8. Two minds are always better than one

9. Create decisions on facts not rumors.

10. Enhancement is not made from a squared room.

[Learn more here: (The 10 Basic Kaizen Principles http:// okkimonosblog.com/accessed 15th May 2018)]

CHAPTER SEVEN

GENERAL LESSONS FROM ALL FACULTIES

PRELIMINARY

1. Be driven by love, vision and the desire to see the kingdom of God expand in relating and working with others.

2. You will not succeed in life unless you are connected to people.

3. Apart from God and your vision, the next thing is people who will help you succeed. Helpers (people) come before money.

4. If you are not accessible you cannot relate with others well enough to succeed with them.

5. Your dream is connected to people.

6. Just as others need what you contain, so you need what others contain.

7. Goals and dreams last longer than rejection, injury and pain. Therefore be willing to endure pain to create and enjoy an eternity of gain through working with others. Do not be scared of hurts, they won't kill you. Be motivated and driven by the assignment.

8. Fill your heart with love for your team mates. Let your heart reach to them in prayer daily to the Almighty God, and your relationship with them will be fantastic and richly rewarding.

9. Close your ears to gossips about your team mate's personal life and what people say they said.

10. Be willing to help your team mates recover from their weaknesses and failures, remembering that you too do fail at times, and is still pursuing perfection.

11. Keep your eyes on the assignment and not on the leadership position.

12. Do not be envious of another. Just play your part, and you will celebrate the success as a team. Knowing that your labor of love is not in vain, keep your hands on the plough and work with all your might until the work is done.

INTERMEDIATE

1. Our minds are not prison but for some, they have made their own minds their prison as they allow their minds to be eaten up by emotions.

2. Your toughts of how you want to live your life will determine how life can be lived.

3. Happiness and Contentment are results of positivity. While sadness and bitterness are for negativity.

4. When someone has not forgiven the past, the mind will become a man's prison

5. It is true that our emotions make us weak when uncontrolled, this makes you cut yourself off from the people who wants to connect with you.

6. It is important to balance how much of the past you cannot let go. We might not forget but we should learn to accept and forgive the past.

7. Just as how much the past leaves us lessons and makes us a better person. It also teaches us to have a heart of stone. An understanding on this and how much you can take and balance will definitely be helpful in living the present.

8. The pain that we feel are the results of the things our mind thinks has broken us. But when you stop the thought, surely the pain will not be there anymore. Learn to absorb the pain until it hurts no more.

[More of this from http://www.jfoutreach.org/archives/archives/ forgetthepastandfocusonwhereyouaregoing.pdf]

BENEFITS OF STUDIES FROM FACULTIES OF INSECTS

1. It enhances productivity.

2. It increases speed.

3. It boosts the morals of all involved in the team – the knowledge that you are not alone encourages, motivates and strengthens the faith of all concerned in accomplishing the assignment.

4. You share the burden and problems of the assignment together.

5. You can defend each other from enemies and all that seek to stop you.

6. Your knowledge and experience will increase as you learn and work with your colleagues and team mates.

7. You will climb the ladder of success faster as you, together as a team share the reward of working as a team.

8. Success, honor, fame, wealth and promotions will be your portion.

WELCOME TO THE UNIVERSITY OF INSECTS. I HOPE YOU WILL LEARN AS MUCH AS IS AVAILABLE AND GRADUATE WITH A FIRST CLASS!
GOD BLESS YOU!

Printed in the United States
By Bookmasters